girls
can
too!

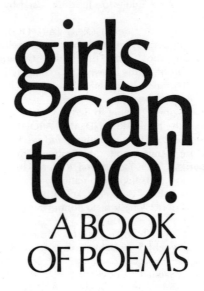

girls can too!
A BOOK OF POEMS

selected by Lee Bennett Hopkins
illustrated by Emily McCully

FRANKLIN WATTS INC.
NEW YORK / 1972

ACKNOWLEDGMENTS:

Thanks are due to the following authors, publishers, and agents for permission to use the material included:

Atheneum Publishers, Inc., for "Horseback Ride" and "Broken Leg" from FEATHER IN MY HAND. Text copyright © 1967 by Siddie Joe Johnson. Used by permission of Atheneum Publishers.

Thomas Y. Crowell Company, for "June" from GOING BAREFOOT. Text copyright © 1960 by Aileen Fisher. Reprinted with permission of Thomas Y. Crowell Co., Inc.

Curtis Brown, Ltd., for "Girls Can, Too!" and "Tricia's Fish." Copyright © 1972 by Lee Bennett Hopkins. Used by permission of Curtis Brown, Ltd. "Naughty Donna." Copyright © 1971 by Lee Bennett Hopkins. Reprinted by permission of Curtis Brown, Ltd. This poem first appeared in *Humpty Dumpty's Magazine.*

E. P. Dutton & Co., Inc., for the poem "Going to Bed" by Marchette Chute. Copyright, 1941, by Marchette Chute. From the book AROUND AND ABOUT by Marchette Chute. Copyright, 1957, by E. P. Dutton & Co., Inc., publishers, and used with their permission.

Follett Publishing Company, for "Angry" and "My Brother" from THAT WAS SUMMER by Marci Ridlon. Text copyright © 1969 by Marci Ridlon. Used by permission of Follett Publishing Company, division of Follett Corporation.

Harcourt Brace Jovanovich, Inc., for "Wide Awake" from WIDE AWAKE AND OTHER POEMS, © 1959, by Myra Cohn Livingston. Reprinted by permission of Harcourt Brace Jovanovich, Inc.

Harper & Row, Publishers, Inc., for "I Woke Up This Morning" from THE ROSE ON MY CAKE by Karla Kuskin. Copyright © 1964 by Karla Kuskin. Reprinted by permission of Harper & Row, Publishers.

Bobbi Katz, for "Oh Suzy" and "Samuel." Copyright © 1972 by Bobbi Katz.

J. B. Lippincott Company, for "Ann" from the book SPEAKING OF COWS by Kaye Starbird. Copyright © 1960 by Kaye Starbird. Reprinted by permission of J. B. Lippincott Company.

Little, Brown and Company, for "Every Time I Climb a Tree" from FAR AND FEW by David McCord. Copyright, 1952, by David McCord. By permission of Little, Brown and Company.

G. P. Putnam's Sons, for "Inch Worm" and "See, I Can Do It" from ALL TOGETHER by Dorothy Aldis. Copyright 1925, 1926, 1927, 1928, 1934, 1939 and 1952 by Dorothy Aldis. By permission of G. P. Putnam's Sons.

Melanie Ray, for "Bea's Bee" and "My Turn." Copyright © 1972 by Melanie Ray. Used by permission.

Library of Congress Cataloging in Publication Data

Hopkins, Lee Bennett, comp.
    Girls can, too!

    SUMMARY: These poems testify to the fact that girls do things as well as boys if not better.
    1. Children's poetry (Collections) [1. Girls—Poetry] I. McCully, Emily Arnold, illus. II. Title.
PZ8.3.H776Gi   811'.5'4080352   72-887
ISBN 0-531-02587-X

CONTENTS

girls
can
too!

WIDE AWAKE

Myra Cohn Livingston

I have to jump up
    out of bed
    and stretch my hands
    and rub my head,
    and curl my toes
    and yawn
    and shake
    myself
    all wide-awake!

MY TURN

Melanie Ray

Kenny always beats me
to the breakfast table

and he always eats
the very first pancake

and he always sits
closest to the maple syrup.

Today, I got up first
and beat him to everything

—even the hot chocolate!

11

MY BROTHER

Marci Ridlon

My brother's worth about two cents,
As far as I can see.
I simply cannot understand
Why they would want a "he."

He spends a good part of his day
Asleep inside the crib,
And when he eats, he has to wear
A stupid baby bib.

He cannot walk and cannot talk
And cannot throw a ball.
In fact, he can't do anything—
He's just no fun at all.

It would have been more sensible,
As far as I can see,
Instead of getting one like him
To get one just like me.

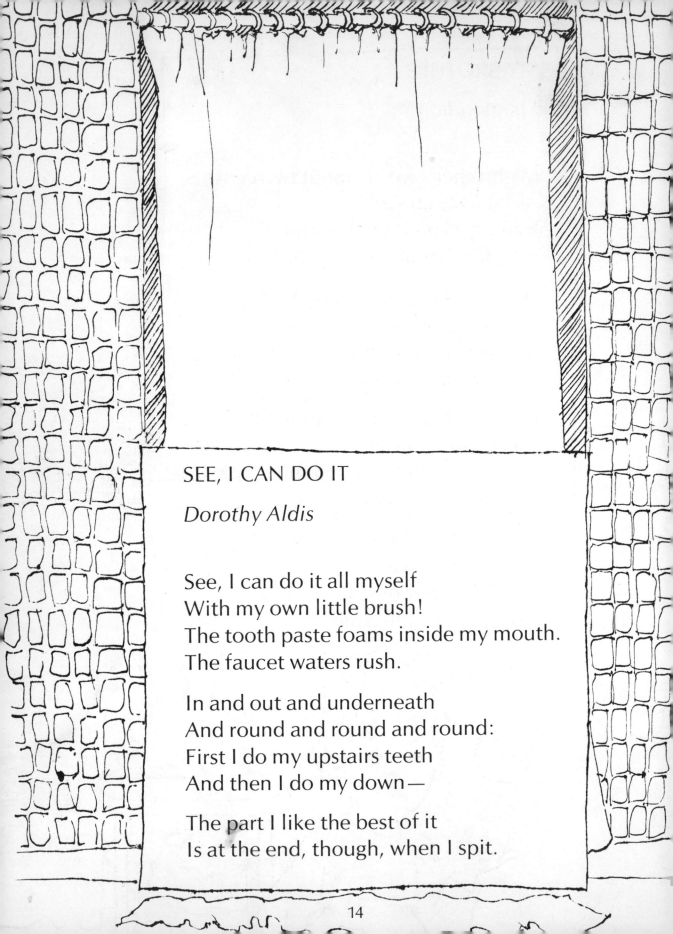

SEE, I CAN DO IT

Dorothy Aldis

See, I can do it all myself
With my own little brush!
The tooth paste foams inside my mouth.
The faucet waters rush.

In and out and underneath
And round and round and round:
First I do my upstairs teeth
And then I do my down—

The part I like the best of it
Is at the end, though, when I spit.

BEA'S BEE

Melanie Ray

Boy! Is everyone proud of me!
Today I won the spelling bee!
Nobody thought I really could—
Even though I knew I would.
I practiced hard to beat the rest,
Even Michael who's always best.

I learned to spell *duckling*, and *forty-three*,
And *ribbons* and *toothpaste* and *honeybee*.
Whistle finally did Michael in.

Wow! He was mad 'cause he didn't win.
Now I tell everyone, and it's all true,
That anything he can do,
I can do, too!

SAMUEL

Bobbi Katz

I found this salamander
Near the pond in the wood.

    Samuel, I called him—
    Samuel, Samuel.

Right away I loved him.
He loved me too, I think.

    Samuel, I called him—
    Samuel, Samuel.

I took him home in a coffee can,
And at night
He slept in my bed.

In the morning
I took him to school.

He died very quietly during spelling.

Sometimes I think
I should have left him
Near the pond in the woods.

    Samuel, I called him—
    Samuel, Samuel.

INCH-WORM

Dorothy Aldis

Little green inch-worm,
Inch-worm, inch.
You can't hurt me,
You don't pinch.
Never did anyone
Any harm
So *take* your little green walk
Up my arm.

ANN

Kaye Starbird

Ann wears dresses with ruffles,
If you please.
And she *won't* wear dungarees.
She has neat, curly hair
And a real gold ring,
—And she can't play *anything*.

You say to her,
"Be a cow,"
And she doesn't know how.
Or else you rush around,
Shouting, "Let's be cops!"
—She runs for a while,
Then stops.
Just as you track the thieves
With none of them knowing,
She hollers
"Where are we going?"

The times you whisper,
"Look at that ambush there,"
She wants to know
What bush
Where?

Faced with a simple game
Like wolves on the prowl,
She won't even howl.

Ann is clean,
And she always carries a comb.
And I *wish*
She'd stay home.

OH, SUZY

Bobbi Katz

Oh Suzy,
Roughy-toughy-Suzy-friend,
Why did you move away?
Other girls do stupid stuff
Like playing dumb old house
And dressing their creepy dolls,
No one wants to wrestle
Or roll down hills—

over
    and
        over—
            so
                many
                    overs.

Oh Suzy,
Roughy-toughy-Suzy friend,
Why did you move away?

GIRLS CAN, TOO!

Lee Bennett Hopkins

Tony said: "Boys are better!
  They can...

    whack a ball,
    ride a bike with one hand
    leap off a wall."

I just listened
  and when he was through,
I laughed and said:

  "Oh, yeah! Well girls can, too!"

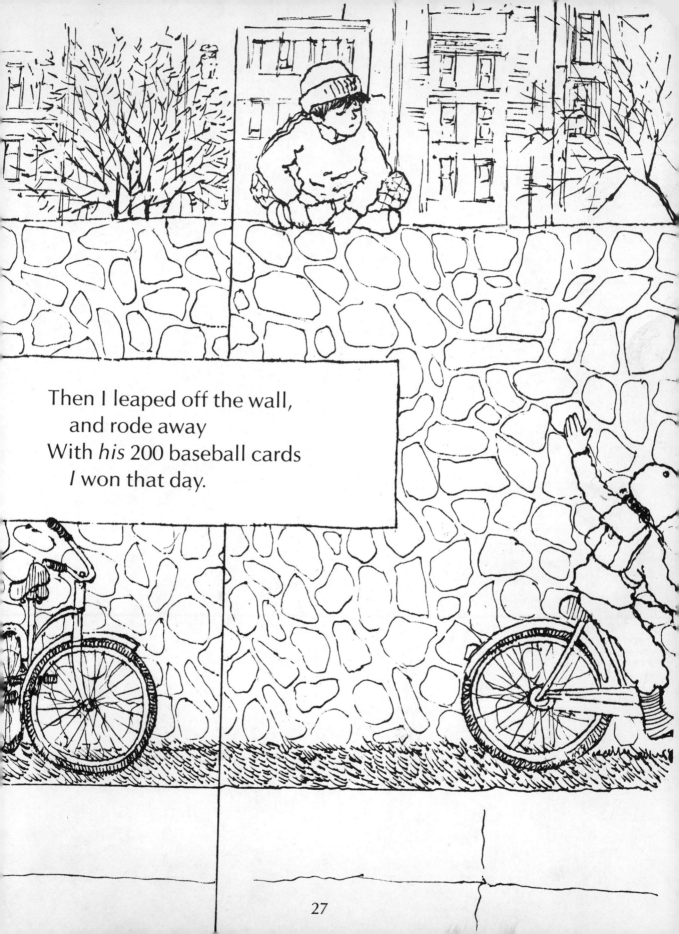

Then I leaped off the wall,
 and rode away
With *his* 200 baseball cards
 I won that day.

JUNE

Aileen Fisher

The day is warm
and a breeze is blowing,
the sky is blue
and its eye is glowing,
and everything's new
and green and growing....

My shoes are off
and my socks are showing....

My socks are off....

Do you know how I'm going?
  BAREFOOT!

HORSEBACK RIDE

Siddie Joe Johnson

Old Nellie is so very high,
I am a little scared to be
Up in the sky on top of her,
With Gilly and Ann in back of me.

But when she starts to gallop some,
I close my eyes and travel free,
Nothing else in the world but us—
No one by but the wind to see
How we go flying down the field,
Nellie and Gilly and Ann and me.

TRICIA'S FISH

Lee Bennett Hopkins

Whenever I go fishing
I keep on wishing
I wouldn't catch so *many*!

Because—

Ralph and Ron and Ricky,
Martha, Marge and Mickie

don't
    ever, ever
        catch any!

EVERY TIME I CLIMB A TREE

David McCord

Every time I climb a tree
Every time I climb a tree
Every time I climb a tree
I scrape a leg
Or skin a knee
And every time I climb a tree
I find some ants
Or dodge a bee
And get the ants
All over me

And every time I climb a tree
Where have you been?
They say to me
But don't they know that I am free
Every time I climb a tree?
I like it best
To spot a nest
That has an egg
Or maybe three

And then I skin
The other leg
But every time I climb a tree
I see a lot of things to see
Swallows, rooftops and TV
And all the fields and farms there be
Every time I climb a tree
Though climbing may be good for ants
It isn't awfully good for pants
But still it's pretty good for me
Every time I climb a tree

BROKEN LEG

Siddie Joe Johnson

I feel almost as though I were an egg,
My shell not quite hatched through,
With all this clumsy cast upon my leg.
If only I had been a hatching robin,
At least my shell would be a lovely speckled blue

And my small hope of ever coming free
Seem nearer true.

NAUGHTY DONNA

Lee Bennett Hopkins

I like getting toys that will
   make lots of noise—
Especially the kind
That will *scare* all the boys!

ANGRY

Marci Ridlon

Sometimes when the day is bad
And someone's made me very mad
Or I've been given angry stares,
I go behind the front porch stairs.

There, curled up with chin on knee,
I like to be alone with me
And listen to the people talk
And hurry by me on the walk.

There I sit without a sound,
And draw stick pictures on the ground.
If I should tire of it all,
I throw some pebbles at the wall.

After I've been there awhile
And find that I can almost smile,
I brush me off and count to ten
And try to start the day again.

GOING TO BED

Marchette Chute

I'm always told to hurry up —
   Which I'd be glad to do,
If there were not so many things
   That need attending to.

But first I have to find my towel
   Which fell behind the rack,
And when a pillow's thrown at me
   I have to throw it back.

And then I have to get the things
   I need in bed with me.
Like marbles and my birthday train
   And Pete the chimpanzee.

I have to see my polliwog
   Is safely in its pan,
And stand a minute on my head
   To be quite sure I can.

I have to bounce upon my bed
   To see if it will sink,
And then when I am covered up
   I find I need a drink.

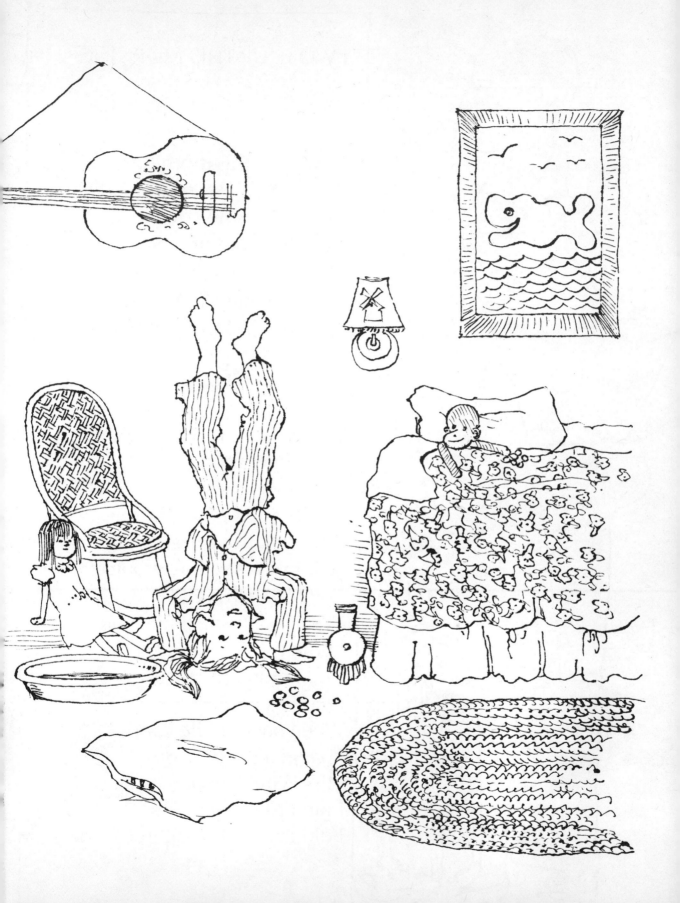

I WOKE UP THIS MORNING

Karla Kuskin

I woke up this morning
At quarter past seven.
I kicked up the covers
And stuck out my toe.
And ever since then
(That's a quarter past seven)
They haven't said anything
Other than "no."
They haven't said anything
Other than "Please, dear,
Don't do what you're doing,"
Or "Lower your voice."
Whatever I've done
And however I've chosen,
I've done the wrong thing
And I've made the wrong choice.
I didn't wash well
And I didn't say thank you.
I didn't shake hands
And I didn't say please.
I didn't say sorry
When passing the candy.
I banged the box into
Miss Witelson's knees.
I didn't say sorry.
I didn't stand straighter.

I didn't speak louder
When asked what I'd said.
Well, I said
That tomorrow
At quarter past seven
They can
Come in and get me
I'm Staying In Bed.

ABOUT THE AUTHOR

There are few people around today who can match Lee Bennett Hopkins either in his knowledge of or in his love of children's poetry. While Mr. Hopkins works full-time as Curriculum and Editorial Specialist for Scholastic Magazines, he still manages to conduct popular poetry seminars all over the United States and to teach part time at a New York City university. He is a graduate of Bank Street College and Hunter College. Mr. Hopkins has written numerous books, dozens of magazine articles, and he has edited a number of fine anthologies, including *The City Spreads Its Wings,* which also was published by Franklin Watts, Inc., and which, like *Girls Can Too!,* includes original poetry by Lee Bennett Hopkins.

ABOUT THE ARTIST

Emily Arnold McCully has illustrated a number of fine books, including *Maxie, Go and Hush the Baby, Journey from Peppermint Street* (National Book Award winner, 1968), *Steffie and Me,* and *Henry's Pennies.* Mrs. McCully is a graduate of Brown and Columbia universities. She lives with her husband and two sons.